AF316770

SECRETS AND SEDUCTION

Secrets and Seduction

A Guide for Affair Partners

LOUIS MALONE

Advise the Heart

CONTENTS

~ 5 ~

Moving Forward and Making Decisions

~ 6 ~

Embracing Self-Care and Personal Growth

~ 7 ~

Conclusion

Copyright © 2024 by Advise the Heart, an imprint of Bald and Bonkers Network LLC

All rights reserved. No part of this book may be reproduced in any manner whatsoever without written permission except in the case of brief quotations embodied in critical articles and reviews.

First Printing, 2024

ISBN/: 979-8-8692-7300-0
EISBN: 979-8-8692-7301-7

~ 1 ~

UNDERSTANDING YOUR ROLE AS THE "OTHER PERSON"

The Stigma of Being the "Other Woman" or "Other Man"

The role of being the "other woman" or "other man" in a relationship often carries a significant stigma and societal judgment. Those who find themselves as affair partners may face criticism and shame, feeling isolated due to the guilt and immorality associated with their label.

In many societies, affairs are viewed as taboo

and morally reprehensible, casting those involved with married or emotionally unavailable partners as villains in the narrative. This perception can significantly impact the mental and emotional health of affair partners, fostering guilt, shame, and self-doubt.

However, it's crucial for those in such relationships to understand they are not alone. Relationships with married or emotionally unavailable partners happen for myriad reasons, and the issues are rarely clear-cut. Comprehending the intricacies of human relationships and emotions is key to managing the complexities they entail.

"Secrets and Seduction: A Guide for Affair Partners" delves into the stigma surrounding the roles of "other" partners and offers support and advice for managing these challenging dynamics. The guide seeks to counteract societal judgments and the internalized shame felt by affair partners, aiding them in finding validation and understanding. It's essential to remember that societal labels do not define an individual's entire being; everyone is deserving of love and respect, regardless of their circumstances.

Embracing Your Role in the Affair

In the tumultuous world of affairs, it can be easy to lose sight of your role and purpose as the "other person." However, embracing your role in the affair is essential for maintaining a sense of control and understanding in what can often be a chaotic and emotionally charged situation.

As an affair partner, it's important to acknowledge and accept the reality of your position. You are not the primary partner in this relationship, and you may never be. Understanding and coming to terms with this fact can help you navigate the complexities of your involvement with more clarity and self-awareness.

Embracing your role also means setting boundaries and expectations for yourself within the affair. Clearly defining what you are willing to accept and what you are not can help you avoid getting swept up in the emotional roller-coaster that often accompanies affairs. It's important to remember that you have agency and control over your own actions and decisions, even in the midst of a passionate and intense affair.

Additionally, embracing your role in the affair involves taking responsibility for your own emotions and desires. It can be easy to get caught up in the thrill of a forbidden romance, but it's important to remember that affairs are inherently risky and can have serious consequences for all involved. By acknowledging your own vulnerabilities and motivations, you can better understand why you are drawn to this particular situation and make more informed choices moving forward.

Ultimately, embracing your role in the affair means accepting the reality of the situation while also staying true to yourself and your own values. By approaching the affair with honesty, self-awareness, and clarity, you can navigate this complex and often challenging relationship with grace and integrity.

Managing Your Expectations in a Secret Relationship

When engaging in a secret relationship, it is important to be mindful of your expectations. As an affair partner, you may find yourself in a complex and emotionally charged situation that can be both exhilarating and challenging. It is crucial to understand and acknowledge the limitations and boundaries of a secret relationship to avoid disappointment and heartache.

First and foremost, it is essential to recognize that a secret relationship is inherently risky and unstable. Affairs with married individuals or emotionally unavailable partners come with a set of unique challenges that can make it difficult to maintain a sense of stability and security. It is important to be realistic about the nature of the relationship and to accept that it may not always meet your emotional or physical needs.

Managing your expectations also involves being prepared for the possibility of secrecy and discretion. As an affair partner, you may need to adjust your expectations regarding communication, availability, and public displays of affection. It is important to understand that your relationship may need to remain hidden from others, which can impact the level of intimacy and connection you are able to share.

Additionally, it is crucial to establish clear boundaries and expectations with your affair partner. Communication is key in any relationship, but it is especially important in a secret relationship where honesty and transparency may be limited. Make sure to have open and honest conversations about your needs, desires, and limitations to ensure that both partners are on the same page.

In conclusion, managing your expectations in a secret relationship requires honesty, communication, and a realistic understanding of the challenges that come with being the "other person." By setting boundaries, being prepared for secrecy, and maintaining open communication, you can navigate the complexities of a secret relationship with grace and awareness.

~ 2 ~

NAVIGATING AFFAIRS WITH MARRIED INDIVIDUALS

Recognizing the Risks and Consequences

As affair partners, it is crucial to understand and acknowledge the potential risks and consequences that come with engaging in a relationship with a married or otherwise unavailable individual. While the allure of forbidden love and emotional intimacy may be strong, it is important to consider the impact that your actions could have on all parties involved.

One of the most significant risks of being in a relationship as the "other person" is the potential for emotional turmoil and heartbreak. Being in a relationship with someone who is unable to fully commit to you can lead to feelings of insecurity, jealousy, and loneliness. It can be incredibly challenging to navigate the complexities of a relationship where you are not the primary partner, and the emotional toll can be significant.

Furthermore, there are practical consequences to consider as well. Engaging in an affair with a married individual can have legal implications, especially if children are involved. It can also lead to social ostracization and damage to your reputation. Additionally, there is always the risk of being caught, which can have devastating consequences for all parties involved.

As emotional affair partners, it is important to be mindful of the impact that your actions can have on your own emotional well-being, as well as the well-being of your partner and their spouse. It is essential to consider whether the potential rewards of the relationship outweigh the risks and consequences.

In the end, recognizing the risks and consequences of engaging in a relationship as the "other person" is crucial for affair partners. By being aware of the potential pitfalls and challenges, you can make more informed decisions about whether to continue the relationship or to seek healthier alternatives. Remember, honesty and communication are key in any relationship, even if it is a forbidden one.

Setting Boundaries in a Relationship with a Married Person

Navigating a relationship with a married person can be a complex and challenging experience. As an affair partner or emotional affairs partner, it is crucial to set boundaries to protect yourself and maintain a sense of integrity in the relationship.

First and foremost, it is important to acknowledge the reality of the situation. Being involved with a married individual means that you are in a relationship that is inherently unequal and potentially harmful to all parties involved. Setting boundaries is essential to ensure that you are not being taken advantage of or putting yourself in a position of emotional vulnerability.

One key boundary to establish is maintaining clear communication with your married partner. Be honest about your feelings and expectations in the relationship, and make sure that both parties are on the same page about the nature of the affair. Setting boundaries around communication can help prevent misunderstandings and ensure that both parties are aware of the limitations of the relationship.

Another important boundary to consider is setting limits on the amount of time and energy you are willing to invest in the affair. It can be easy to become emotionally entangled with a married person, but it is important to prioritize your own well-being and not allow the relationship to consume your life.

Ultimately, setting boundaries in a relationship with a married person is about respecting yourself and your own needs. By establishing clear limits and expectations, you can protect yourself from potential harm and maintain a sense of integrity in the affair. Remember that you deserve to be treated with respect and honesty, even in a relationship that may be considered taboo or unconventional.

Dealing with Guilt and Shame in a Forbidden Romance

Navigating the complex emotions of guilt and shame in a forbidden romance can be overwhelming for affair partners and emotional affair partners. The societal stigma attached to being the "other person" in a relationship can lead to feelings of self-blame and worthlessness. However, it is crucial to address these emotions in order to maintain a healthy mindset and approach towards the affair.

First and foremost, it is important to acknowledge and accept the feelings of guilt and shame that may arise in a forbidden romance. These emotions are natural and are often a result of societal norms and expectations. By recognizing these feelings, affair partners can begin to understand the root of their emotions and work towards overcoming them.

One way to deal with guilt and shame in a forbidden romance is to practice self-compassion. Affair partners must remind themselves that they are human beings with valid emotions and desires. By showing kindness and understanding towards oneself, affair partners can begin to let go of the negative feelings associated with their relationship.

Another helpful strategy is to seek support from a trusted friend, therapist, or support group. Talking about feelings of guilt and shame with someone who understands the complexities of a forbidden romance can provide much-needed validation and perspective. Affair partners should not isolate themselves but instead reach out for help when needed.

In conclusion, dealing with guilt and shame in a forbidden romance is a challenging but necessary aspect of maintaining a healthy mindset. By acknowledging these emotions, practicing self-compassion, and seeking support, affair partners can navigate the complexities of their relationship with a renewed sense of understanding and self-acceptance. Remember, you are not alone in your feelings, and there are resources available to help you through this difficult time.

~ 3 ~

EMOTIONAL AFFAIRS WITH UNAVAILABLE PARTNERS

Understanding the Dynamics of an Emotional Affair

In this subchapter, we will delve into the complex dynamics of an emotional affair, exploring the unique challenges and consequences that come with being involved in a relationship with someone who is already committed to another.

First and foremost, it is important to understand that emotional affairs are not just about physical intimacy, but rather about forming a deep emotional connection with someone outside of your primary relationship. This can often lead to feelings of betrayal, guilt, and confusion for both parties involved.

It is crucial for affair partners to recognize the impact that their actions can have on not only their own lives, but also the lives of their partner's spouse and family. By acknowledging the emotional consequences of their actions, affair partners can begin to navigate the complexities of their relationship in a more mindful and responsible manner.

Furthermore, it is essential for affair partners to communicate openly and honestly with each other about their feelings and intentions. By maintaining clear boundaries and expectations, both parties can better understand the nature of their relationship and avoid unnecessary misunderstandings and hurt feelings.

Ultimately, understanding the dynamics of an emotional affair requires a deep sense of self-awareness and emotional intelligence. By reflecting on the motivations behind their actions and the impact they have on others, affair partners can begin to navigate the complexities of their relationship in a more compassionate and respectful manner.

In the end, it is crucial for affair partners to approach their relationship with empathy, honesty, and integrity, in order to minimize the harm caused to themselves and others involved. By understanding the dynamics of an emotional affair, affair partners can begin to make more informed and ethical decisions about their relationship moving forward.

Communicating with an Emotionally Unavailable Partner

One of the biggest challenges faced by affair partners in emotional affairs is trying to communicate with an emotionally unavailable partner. When you are involved with someone who is married or otherwise committed, their emotional unavailability can make it difficult to connect on a deeper level. However, there are strategies you can use to improve communication and strengthen your bond with an emotionally unavailable partner.

First and foremost, it is important to remember that you cannot force someone to open up emotionally if they are not ready or willing to do so. It is essential to be patient and understanding, and to give your partner the space they need to work through their emotions at their own pace. Avoid putting pressure on them to open up or share more than they are comfortable with.

In order to improve communication with an emotionally unavailable partner, it is crucial to create a safe and non-judgmental environment. Encourage your partner to express their feelings and thoughts without fear of criticism or rejection. Listen actively and attentively, and try to understand their perspective without jumping to conclusions or making assumptions.

Another effective strategy for communicating with an emotionally unavailable partner is to focus on building trust and establishing a strong emotional connection. Share your own feelings and vulnerabilities, and encourage your partner to do the same. By creating a sense of mutual trust and understanding, you can help your partner feel more comfortable opening up and expressing their emotions.

In conclusion, communicating with an emotionally unavailable partner in an affair requires patience, understanding, and a willingness to create a safe and supportive environment. By following these strategies and working together to build trust and emotional intimacy, you can strengthen your bond with your partner and navigate the challenges of an emotional affair with grace and empathy.

Coping with the Emotional Intensity of a Secret Relationship

Being in a secret relationship can be incredibly intense and overwhelming. The emotional rollercoaster of being involved with someone who is unavailable can take a toll on your mental and emotional well-being. As affair partners, it is important to recognize and acknowledge the emotional challenges that come with this type of relationship.

First and foremost, it is crucial to understand that the secrecy and forbidden nature of the relationship can create a sense of guilt, shame, and loneliness. It is natural to feel conflicted about your feelings for your partner and the impact it may have on their marriage or relationship. It is important to find healthy ways to cope with these emotions, such as seeking support from a therapist or confiding in a trusted friend.

Additionally, the constant fear of being discovered can lead to anxiety and stress. It is important to establish boundaries and communication with your partner to minimize the risk of being caught. Setting realistic expectations and discussing the potential consequences of the relationship can help alleviate some of the anxiety.

Moreover, managing expectations and understanding the limitations of a secret relationship is essential. It is important to recognize that your partner may not be able to fully commit to you due to their existing commitments. It is crucial to prioritize self-care and focus on your own emotional well-being.

In conclusion, coping with the emotional intensity of a secret relationship requires self-awareness, communication, and self-care. It is important to acknowledge the challenges that come with being an affair partner and find healthy ways to navigate the complexities of this type of relationship. Remember to prioritize your own emotional well-being and seek support when needed.

~ 4 ~

COPING WITH THE CHALLENGES OF BEING AN AFFAIR PARTNER

Dealing with Jealousy and Insecurity

Dealing with jealousy and insecurity is a common challenge for affair partners. When you are in a relationship with a married individual or an emotionally unavailable partner, it can be easy to feel insecure about your place in their life. You may worry about their commitment to you, or feel jealous of their spouse or other relationships they have.

One of the first steps in dealing with jealousy and insecurity is to acknowledge and accept your feelings. It is normal to feel these emotions in a relationship that is inherently complicated and often secretive. By recognizing and accepting your feelings, you can begin to address them in a healthy way.

Communication is key when it comes to dealing with jealousy and insecurity in an affair. Talk to your partner about your feelings and concerns, and listen to their perspective as well. Open and honest communication can help build trust and strengthen your relationship.

It is also important to focus on building your own self-confidence and self-worth. Remember that you are worthy of love and respect, regardless of your relationship status. Take time to engage in activities that make you feel good about yourself, whether it's pursuing a hobby or spending time with friends who support you.

Finally, consider seeking support from a

therapist or counselor who specializes in relationships and affairs. A professional can help you explore and understand your feelings of jealousy and insecurity, and provide guidance on how to navigate these challenging emotions.

By acknowledging your feelings, communicating openly with your partner, building your self-confidence, and seeking support when needed, you can effectively deal with jealousy and insecurity in your affair. Remember that you deserve to be in a healthy, fulfilling relationship, even if it is unconventional.

Managing the Fear of Being Discovered

One of the biggest challenges that affair partners face is the constant fear of being discovered. The thought of their secret relationship being exposed can be overwhelming and anxiety-inducing. However, it's important to find ways to manage this fear in order to maintain a sense of calm and control in the relationship.

First and foremost, it's crucial to establish

clear boundaries and communication with your partner. Discuss the potential risks of being discovered and come up with a plan for how to handle any potential fallout. By being on the same page and having a solid plan in place, you can alleviate some of the anxiety surrounding the fear of being discovered.

Additionally, it's important to take steps to protect your privacy and maintain discretion in your relationship. Avoid leaving any digital traces of your affair, such as text messages or emails, and be cautious about where and when you meet up with your partner. By being mindful of your actions and surroundings, you can reduce the chances of being discovered.

It's also beneficial to seek support from others who understand your situation, such as fellow affair partners or therapists specializing in relationships with unavailable partners. Having a support system in place can help you navigate the challenges of managing the fear of being discovered and provide a sense of solidarity and understanding.

Ultimately, managing the fear of being discovered requires a combination of communication, boundary-setting, discretion, and support. By taking proactive steps to address this fear, you can focus on enjoying your relationship without constantly looking over your shoulder."

Finding Support and Community as an Affair Partner

Finding support and community as an affair partner can be a challenging and isolating experience. As an affair partner, you may feel like you have to keep your relationship a secret from friends and family, leading to feelings of loneliness and guilt. However, it is important to remember that you are not alone in this situation.

One way to find support and community as an affair partner is to connect with others who are in similar situations. There are online forums and support groups specifically for affair partners where you can share your experiences, seek advice, and find understanding from people who are going through the same thing. These online communities can provide a sense of belonging and validation that may be lacking in your everyday life.

It is also important to surround yourself with understanding and non-judgmental friends or confidants who can support you through this difficult time. While it may be tempting to confide in someone who may not understand or approve of your choices, having a support system that accepts you for who you are can make a world of difference.

Additionally, seeking therapy or counseling can be beneficial for affair partners seeking support and guidance. A therapist can help you navigate the complex emotions and ethical dilemmas that may arise in an affair, and provide you with tools to cope with stress and guilt.

Remember, finding support and community as an affair partner is essential for your emotional well-being. By connecting with others who understand your situation and seeking professional help when needed, you can navigate the challenges of being the "other person" in a relationship with more confidence and self-awareness.

~ 5 ~

MOVING FORWARD
AND MAKING
DECISIONS

Evaluating the Future of Your Relationship

Assessing the future of a relationship is a critical step for those involved in emotional affairs, particularly with married or otherwise committed individuals. This section offers guidance on evaluating your relationship's potential and making well-informed choices about its direction.

Key to this evaluation is the degree of commitment and transparency between partners.

It's vital to ask: Are both parties ready to openly share their feelings and intentions? Have boundaries been established to safeguard each person's emotional health? Reflecting on these questions is fundamental to understanding the relationship's trajectory.

Moreover, examining long-term compatibility is essential. Do you and your partner hold shared values, objectives, and visions for the future? Are there substantial challenges or disparities that could impede your relationship's progress? Open and honest dialogue regarding these issues is imperative to ensure mutual understanding and agreement.

Additionally, one must contemplate the repercussions of maintaining the relationship. What risks are involved, including possible emotional harm, reputational damage, or legal complications? These considerations must be weighed judiciously to make choices that resonate with your principles and life goals.

In conclusion, determining the future of

your relationship demands candid communication, introspection, and a commitment to prioritize emotional health. By dedicating time to evaluate your relationship's potential, you can arrive at decisions that foster a healthier, more satisfying partnership.

Considering the Impact on Other People Involved

When engaging in an affair, it is essential to consider the impact on other people involved. Whether you are the "other person" in a relationship, having an affair with a married individual, or engaging in an emotional affair with an unavailable partner, there are consequences that extend beyond just the two people directly involved.

First and foremost, it is crucial to recognize that the person you are having an affair with has a significant other who is likely unaware of the situation. This can cause immense pain and heartbreak for the betrayed partner, leading to feelings of betrayal, anger, and hurt.

It is important to consider the impact of your actions on this individual and the ripple effect it can have on their lives.

Additionally, if children are involved, the consequences of an affair can be even more far-reaching. Children can be deeply affected by infidelity in their parents' relationship, causing emotional trauma and long-lasting effects on their well-being. By engaging in an affair, you are not only hurting the betrayed partner but also potentially harming innocent children who have no control over the situation.

Furthermore, consider the impact on your own emotional well-being and reputation. Engaging in an affair can lead to feelings of guilt, shame, and regret, which can take a toll on your mental health and overall happiness. Additionally, your actions may have lasting consequences on your reputation and relationships with others, as infidelity can tarnish your character and integrity.

In conclusion, when considering engaging in

an affair, it is essential to think about the impact on other people involved. By taking into account the feelings of the betrayed partner, children, and even yourself, you can make a more informed decision about whether or not to pursue a relationship outside of your current commitments. Remember that the consequences of infidelity can be significant and far-reaching, so tread carefully and consider the potential repercussions before proceeding.

Exploring the Possibility of Ending the Affair or Taking It to the Next Level

As affair partners, it is essential to consider the direction in which your relationship is heading. Are you content with the current state of your affair, or are you beginning to feel the need for a change? This subchapter will help you navigate the complexities of deciding whether to end the affair or take it to the next level.

Ending the affair can be a daunting prospect, especially if you have developed strong emotional connections with your partner. It is crucial to evaluate your reasons for wanting to end the affair. Are you feeling guilty about being the "other person"? Are you no longer satisfied with the secrecy and lies that come with an affair? It is important to be honest with yourself and your partner about your feelings and intentions.

On the other hand, taking the affair to the next level can also be a challenging decision to make. Are you both prepared to leave your current relationships and pursue a future together? Have you discussed the potential consequences of making your affair public? It is crucial to have open and honest communication with your partner about your desires and expectations for the future of your relationship.

Ultimately, the decision to end the affair or take it to the next level should be made with careful consideration of your own emotions and the potential impact on all parties involved. Remember to prioritize your emotional well-being and be prepared for the consequences of your actions. Whether you choose to end the affair or take it to the next level, it is essential to approach the situation with honesty, empathy, and respect for yourself and your partner.

~ 6 ~

EMBRACING SELF-CARE AND PERSONAL GROWTH

Prioritizing Your Emotional Well-Being

As an affair partner, navigating the complex emotions and dynamics of being involved with a married individual or an unavailable partner can take a toll on your emotional well-being. It is essential to prioritize your mental and emotional health to ensure that you are able to handle the challenges that may arise in this type of relationship.

One of the first steps in prioritizing your emotional well-being is to acknowledge and validate your feelings. It is natural to experience a range of emotions, including guilt, shame, excitement, and confusion, when involved in an affair. By recognizing and accepting these emotions, you can begin to understand the underlying reasons for your actions and work towards finding peace within yourself.

Setting boundaries is another crucial aspect of prioritizing your emotional well-being as an affair partner. Establishing clear boundaries with your partner and yourself can help protect your feelings and prevent you from becoming too emotionally invested in a relationship that may not have a future. It is important to communicate your needs and expectations openly and honestly to ensure that both parties are on the same page.

Additionally, seeking support from a therapist or counselor can be beneficial in helping you process your emotions and gain a deeper understanding of yourself. Therapy can provide a safe space for you to explore your feelings, address any underlying issues that may be contributing to your involvement in an affair, and develop healthy coping mechanisms.

Ultimately, prioritizing your emotional well-being as an affair partner is essential for maintaining your mental health and overall happiness. By acknowledging your feelings, setting boundaries, and seeking support when needed, you can navigate the complexities of being the "other person" in a relationship with more clarity and self-awareness. Remember, your emotional well-being should always come first.

Investing in Your Own Happiness and Fulfillment

As an affair partner, it can be easy to get caught up in the whirlwind of emotions and excitement that comes with being involved with someone who is already committed to another person. However, it is crucial to remember that your own happiness and fulfillment should not solely depend on the relationship you have with your affair partner.

Investing in your own happiness means taking the time to focus on yourself and your own needs. This can involve pursuing your passions, hobbies, and interests outside of the affair. By doing so, you will not only feel more fulfilled as an individual but also less reliant on the affair for your sense of happiness.

It is also important to prioritize self-care and self-love. This can involve setting boundaries in the affair to ensure that your emotional well-being is not compromised. Taking care of yourself physically, mentally, and emotionally will not only benefit you but also the relationship you have with your affair partner.

Additionally, investing in your own happiness and fulfillment can lead to a greater sense of empowerment and self-confidence. By focusing on your own growth and development, you will become a stronger and more independent individual, which can ultimately enhance the dynamics of your relationship with your affair partner.

Remember, you deserve to be happy and fulfilled in all aspects of your life, not just in your relationship with your affair partner. By investing in yourself and prioritizing your own well-being, you will not only improve your own life but also the quality of your relationship with your affair partner.

Reflecting on Lessons Learned from Your Affair Experience

As an affair partner, it is important to take the time to reflect on the lessons learned from your experience. Whether you are involved in a physical affair with a married individual or an emotional affair with an unavailable partner, there are valuable insights to be gained from your actions and choices.

One of the most important lessons to reflect on is the impact of your affair on yourself and others. Consider how your actions have affected your emotional well-being, the well-being of your partner, and any other individuals involved in the affair. Take responsibility for your role in the situation and acknowledge any pain or hurt that has been caused.

Another key lesson to reflect on is the reasons behind your decision to engage in an affair. What was missing in your own relationship that led you to seek fulfillment elsewhere? Were you seeking validation, excitement, or emotional connection that was lacking in your primary partnership? Understanding these underlying motivations can help you address any unresolved issues and make healthier choices in the future.

Reflecting on the dynamics of your affair can also provide valuable insights into patterns of behavior and communication that may have contributed to the affair. Consider how boundaries were crossed, trust was broken, and emotions were manipulated. Identify any warning signs or red flags that you may have ignored and use this knowledge to set healthier boundaries in future relationships.

Ultimately, reflecting on the lessons learned from your affair experience can help you grow and evolve as an individual. By taking the time to examine your actions, motivations, and impact on others, you can gain valuable insights that will guide you towards more fulfilling and authentic relationships in the future.

CONCLUSION

Embracing Your Truth as an Affair Partner

As an affair partner, it is crucial to acknowledge and embrace your truth in order to navigate the complexities of being involved with someone who is already committed to another. This subchapter is dedicated to helping you understand and accept your role in the relationship, while also empowering you to make informed decisions moving forward.

First and foremost, it is important to recognize that being an affair partner can bring about a myriad of conflicting emotions. From guilt and shame to passion and desire, it is natural to experience a whirlwind of feelings when engaging in a relationship with a married individual or an unavailable partner. Embracing your truth means accepting these emotions without judgment, and allowing yourself to explore and understand the reasons behind your involvement in the affair.

Furthermore, embracing your truth as an affair partner involves taking ownership of your actions and decisions. It is essential to communicate openly and honestly with your partner about your needs, desires, and boundaries in the relationship. By being transparent and authentic in your interactions, you can establish a sense of trust and mutual respect that can help navigate the complexities of being the "other person."

Additionally, embracing your truth requires self-reflection and introspection. Take the time to examine your motivations for engaging in an affair, and consider how it aligns with your values and beliefs. By understanding and accepting your own truth, you can make informed decisions about the direction of the relationship and ensure that your needs are being met.

In conclusion, embracing your truth as an affair partner is a journey of self-discovery and empowerment. By acknowledging your emotions, owning your actions, and reflecting on your motivations, you can navigate the complexities of being involved with a married individual or an unavailable partner with confidence and integrity. Remember, your truth is valid, and it deserves to be embraced.

Moving Forward with Clarity and Confidence

As affair partners, it is essential to recognize the complexities and challenges that come with engaging in a relationship with someone who is already committed to another person. The feelings of guilt, uncertainty, and emotional turmoil can often cloud our judgment and leave us feeling lost and confused. However, it is crucial to take a step back and assess the situation with clarity and confidence in order to move forward in a healthy and productive manner.

One of the first steps in moving forward as an affair partner is to acknowledge and accept the reality of the situation. It is important to understand that the relationship you are involved in may not have a future and that there are likely to be many obstacles and challenges along the way. By accepting this truth, you can begin to approach the relationship with a sense of awareness and understanding, rather than blindly following your emotions.

Once you have come to terms with the reality of the affair, it is important to communicate openly and honestly with your partner. Discuss your feelings, desires, and boundaries openly, and make sure that both parties are on the same page regarding the nature of the relationship. By establishing clear communication and boundaries, you can ensure that both partners are aware of each other's needs and expectations, leading to a more harmonious and fulfilling relationship.

Moving forward as an affair partner also requires a strong sense of self-awareness and confidence. It is important to recognize your own worth and value, and to not allow the affair to define your self-esteem. By cultivating a sense of self-assurance and confidence, you can navigate the complexities of the affair with grace and dignity, ultimately leading to a more positive and fulfilling experience.

In conclusion, moving forward as an affair partner requires a combination of clarity, communication, and confidence. By accepting the reality of the situation, communicating openly with your partner, and cultivating self-awareness and confidence, you can navigate the challenges of the affair with grace and dignity. Remember that you deserve to be in a relationship that is fulfilling and respectful, and by approaching the affair with clarity and confidence, you can create a more positive and rewarding experience for both parties involved.

Honoring Your Journey and Your Choices in Love and Relationships

In the complex and often misunderstood world of affairs and emotional entanglements, it is crucial to honor not only the journey you are on, but also the choices you make along the way in love and relationships. As affair partners, emotional affairs partners, and individuals involved in relationships as the "other person," it can be easy to feel guilt, shame, or confusion about the path you have chosen. However, it is important to remember that your choices are valid and deserve to be respected.

One of the first steps in honoring your journey and your choices is to acknowledge and accept your feelings. Whether you are in a relationship with a married individual, involved in an emotional affair with an unavailable partner, or navigating the complexities of being the "other person," your emotions are valid and deserve to be heard. Take the time to explore and understand your feelings without judgment or criticism.

Another important aspect of honoring your journey is to communicate openly and honestly with your partner. Whether you are in a committed affair or an emotional entanglement, it is essential to have open and transparent communication to navigate the challenges and complexities of your relationship. By being honest about your needs, desires, and boundaries, you can create a strong foundation for your partnership.

Finally, remember to prioritize self-care and self-love throughout your journey. It can be easy to lose sight of your own needs and well-being when caught up in the whirlwind of an affair or emotional entanglement. Take the time to prioritize your mental, emotional, and physical health, and remember that you deserve to be loved, respected, and valued in all of your relationships.

By honoring your journey and your choices in love and relationships, you can create a strong and fulfilling partnership that brings joy, passion, and fulfillment to your life. Remember to communicate openly, prioritize self-care, and embrace your feelings with love and acceptance. Your journey is unique and valid, and you deserve to be honored every step of the way.

Printed in the USA
CPSIA information can be obtained
at www.ICGtesting.com
CBHW021522220424
7344CB00003B/25

9 798869 273000